Good
Manners
in Relationships

# Good Manners
# with Your Teachers

by Rebecca Felix

illustrated by Gary LaCoste

**visit us at www.abdopublishing.com**

Published by Magic Wagon, a division of the ABDO Group, PO Box 398166, Minneapolis, MN, 55439. Copyright © 2014 by Abdo Consulting Group, Inc. International copyrights reserved in all countries. All rights reserved. No part of this book may be reproduced in any form without written permission from the publisher.

Looking Glass Library™ is a trademark and logo of Magic Wagon.

Printed in the United States of America, North Mankato, Minnesota.
102013
012014
 The book contains at least 10% recycled materials.

Text by Rebecca Felix
Illustrations by Gary LaCoste
Edited by Stephanie Hedlund and Rochelle Baltzer
Interior layout and design by Renée LaViolette
Cover design by Renée LaViolette

**Library of Congress Cataloging-in-Publication Data**

Felix, Rebecca, 1984-
  Good manners with your teachers / by Rebecca Felix ; illustrated by Gary LaCoste.
      pages cm
  Includes index.
  ISBN 978-1-62402-028-5
1.  Student etiquette.  I. Title.
  BJ1857.S75F45 2014
  395.5--dc23
                            2013031602

# Contents

Why Do Good Manners Matter with Teachers? . . . 4

Show Good Manners with Teachers!. . . . . . . . 10

Manners in Motion . . . . . . . . . . . . . 24

Amazing Facts about Manners with Teachers . . . . 30

Top Five Tips for Good Manners with Teachers . . . 31

Glossary. . . . . . . . . . . . . . . . 31

Web Sites . . . . . . . . . . . . . . . 32

Index . . . . . . . . . . . . . . . . 32

# Why Do Good Manners Matter with Teachers?

Mia is in class.  Her teacher, Mr. Kay, is talking.  He is teaching about the solar system.  This causes Mia to think of the sky.  She stares out the classroom window.  Mia looks at the clouds.  There are many shapes.  Mia wants to draw the clouds.  She takes out her notebook.  Mr. Kay is still talking.  Should Mia draw while he teaches?

Mia should not draw while Mr. Kay teaches. She should listen to the lesson. Paying attention to teachers is good manners. It shows them you are trying to learn. This helps create good relationships with teachers.

What would teacher and student relationships be like without good manners? Mia might doodle every day and ignore Mr. Kay's lessons. Mia's classmates might talk over Mr. Kay.

Students might break classroom rules. They might drink soda or eat snacks in class. These behaviors are rude. They could distract other students. And Mr. Kay would likely become upset.

Just as parents have rules at home, teachers have classroom rules. Following a teacher's rules is good manners.

# Show Good Manners with Teachers!

You are in school many days a week for many years. Showing teachers good manners makes school more pleasant for teachers and for you. It also helps you become a successful student.

Respect is the base of good manners. Showing teachers respect means treating them how you would like to be treated. It means listening. It also means speaking politely. What other manners are important with teachers?

Showing teachers good manners prepares you for success in a job as an adult.

Participation is important to teachers.  It helps students learn.  Teachers expect students to ask questions and answer questions.  Most have rules for doing this.

Mia has a question about a math problem.  To ask it, she should raise her hand.  Then she should wait for her teacher to call on her.  Nate wants to answer a question.  He should also raise his hand and wait to be called on.

A teacher may call on another student to answer a question. If so, it is polite to lower your hand.

Use good manners when you speak with teachers. Nate has trouble playing a note in music class. He can ask his teacher for help. To do this, Nate should use the word "please." It is a "magic word." It makes teachers happy to help you out.

Magic words are short. They are easy to use. But they make a huge difference in communication!

Other magic words to use with teachers include "thank you." Thank teachers after they help you. Nate's music teacher helps him learn the tricky note. Nate should thank her. Thanking teachers shows you appreciate their time, actions, or words.

Teachers might thank you for something. To respond politely, say "you're welcome."

Homework is a big part of being a student. Mr. Kay assigns reading homework. His students are to read a textbook chapter overnight. Mia and Nate should read the correct chapter. This will show that they were listening. It will also mean that they can follow directions. Following directions shows good manners.

Turning homework in on time is part of following directions. This shows teachers that class is important to you. It is also good manners to have books, paper, pens, and pencils ready to use in class. This shows teachers that you are ready to learn.

Everyone makes mistakes. Even teachers! Teachers might also have bad days. It is good manners to show them kindness in these situations.

Mr. Kay accidentally returns a classmate's quiz to Nate. What if Nate yelled at him for the mistake? This behavior would be rude. It might hurt the teacher's feelings. Now get ready to see some good manners in motion!

# Manners in Motion

Mia and Nate's class is working on science posters. Mr. Kay asked students to draw their favorite planet. Then, they are to write their favorite fact about that planet.

Mia draws Saturn.  But she has trouble drawing the planet's rings.  She raises her hand.  Mr. Kay stops over.

"Can you please help me?" Mia asks him.  Mr. Kay shows Mia how to draw the rings.

"Thanks!" she says.

The students finish their posters.  Mr. Kay hangs
them on the wall.  He walks to each poster and
reads the facts aloud to the class.

Nate drew Earth.  His poster is at the end of the line.
Mr. Kay forgets to read it!

Nate raises his hand.  Mr. Kay calls on him.

"I think you forgot to read mine," Nate says.  Mr. Kay apologizes.  Nate says, "That's okay!"

Mr. Kay reads Nate's poster.  His favorite thing about Earth is its people!

How did Mia and Nate show Mr. Kay good manners? They followed directions.  They were polite and kind. Treating teachers this way is easy!  Just remember to show them respect.  What good manners have you practiced with teachers lately?

# Amazing Facts about Manners with Teachers

## Teacher Titles

It is most common for US students to call teachers by their last name. First they place a Ms., Mrs., or Mr. in front. Some teachers might ask to be called by their first name. If so, it is okay to do as they ask. But what if you know a teacher outside of school? For example, if the person is your parent's friend? Or your friend's parent? In school, you should still use whatever name is preferred.

## Reading, Writing, and Respect

In Japan, students are taught education basics similar to anywhere around the world. But there, good manners and respect are especially important. Students in Japan show teachers respect in many ways. They bow to them each morning. They also bow if they see teachers outside of school. During lunch, students serve food to teachers and other students. It is bad manners to take a bite before every person has been served.

# Top Five Tips for Good Manners with Teachers

1. Listen and follow directions.
2. Treat teachers with respect.
3. Be kind.
4. Raise your hand and wait to be called on before speaking.
5. Don't forget to say "please," "thank you," and "excuse me!"

# Glossary

appreciate — to recognize and be thankful for something.

distract — to draw attention away from something else.

participation — the act of taking part in something.

polite — showing good manners by the way you act or speak.

rude — showing bad manners by the way you act or speak.

situation — the event of a certain moment.

successful — having gone well, or as planned.

## Web Sites

To learn more about manners, visit ABDO Group online at **www.abdopublishing.com**. Web sites about manners are featured on our Book Links page. These links are routinely monitored and updated to provide the most current information available.

## Index

answering questions  12
asking questions  12, 14
being kind  22, 28
being polite  10, 28
being prepared  20
classroom rules  8, 12
following directions  18, 20, 28
homework  18, 20
learning  6, 12, 20
listening  6, 10, 18

mistakes  22, 28
participation  12
paying attention  4, 6, 8
please  14, 24
raising your hand  12, 24, 28
respect  10, 28
rude  8, 22
thank you  16, 24
waiting to be called on  12